BODY OF THE WORLD

THE POIEMA POETRY SERIES

Poems are windows into worlds; windows into beauty, goodness, and truth; windows into understandings that won't twist themselves into tidy dogmatic statements; windows into experiences. We can do more than merely peer into such windows; with a little effort we can fling open the casements, and leap over the sills into the heart of these worlds. We are also led into familiar places of hurt, confusion, and disappointment, but we arrive in the poet's company. Poetry is a partnership between poet and reader, seeking together to gain something of value—to get at something important.

Ephesians 2:10 says, "We are God's workmanship..." *poiema* in Greek—the thing that has been made, the masterpiece, the poem. The Poiema Poetry Series presents the work of gifted poets who take Christian faith seriously, and demonstrate in whose image we have been made through their creativity and craftsmanship.

These poets are recent participants in the ancient tradition of David, Asaph, Isaiah, and John the Revelator. The thread can be followed through the centuries—through the diverse poetic visions of Dante, Bernard of Clairvaux, Donne, Herbert, Milton, Hopkins, Eliot, R. S. Thomas, and Denise Levertov—down to the poet whose work is in your hand. With the selection of this volume you are entering this enduring tradition, and as a reader contributing to it.

—D.S. Martin
Series Editor

BODY OF THE WORLD

SARAH ROSSITER

CASCADE *Books* • Eugene, Oregon

BODY OF THE WORLD

Copyright © 2026 Sarah Rossiter. All rights reserved. Except for brief quotations in critical publications or reviews, no part of this book may be reproduced in any manner without prior written permission from the publisher. Write: Permissions, Wipf and Stock Publishers, 199 W. 8th Ave., Suite 3, Eugene, OR 97401.

Cascade Books
An Imprint of Wipf and Stock Publishers
199 W. 8th Ave., Suite 3
Eugene, OR 97401

www.wipfandstock.com

PAPERBACK ISBN: 979-8-3852-4195-8
HARDCOVER ISBN: 979-8-3852-4196-5
EBOOK ISBN: 979-8-3852-4197-2

Cataloguing-in-Publication data:

Names: Rossiter, Sarah, author.

Title: Body of the World: Sarah Rossiter.

Description: Eugene, OR: Cascade Books, 2025 | Poiema Poetry Series

Identifiers: ISBN 979-8-3852-4195-8 (paperback) | ISBN 979-8-3852-4196-5 (hardcover) | ISBN 979-8-3852-4197-2 (ebook)

Subjects: LCSH: Poetry. | Poetry--English language.

Classification: PN1010 R67 2025 (paperback) | PN1010 (ebook)

VERSION NUMBER 01/05/26

To My Beloved Husband
Ned

CONTENTS

I

Plato's Cave 3
White Pelicans 4
Last Week in Jersey City 5
Praying with Luke 6
Excavator 7
Crawlspace 8
Snowdrops 10
Winter Solstice 11
Vernal Pool 12
There is a Field 13
Black Ice 14
Chapel of the Black Madonna 15
The Beautiful Broken 16
Ravines 17
Dispirit 18
Incline Your Ear 19
Rapid River 20
The Last Mattress 21
Maundy Thursday 22
Mourning 23
Green Anole at Middleton Place 24
The Wrens' Lament 25
Marguerite Porete 26

II

Ski Sweater 29

Randall 30

Refuge 31

Semipalmated Sandpipers at Hopewell Cape 32

Summer Place 33

Pieta 34

Stripped 35

On Cutting My Father's Fingernails 36

If the World is too much with You 37

Etty Hillesum 38

Spending the Morning Filling my Fountain Pen 39

Fresh Water 40

Metanoia 41

Mother 42

What The Bones Know 43

How Easy 44

To Feed the Birds 45

Why 46

Horizon 47

Body of the World 48

Fireflies 49

III

Reunion 53

Feather 54

Half-Light 55

After 56

Red Fox 57

Speech 58

Alchemy 59

Slow Work 60

The Other Side 61
Acorns 62
Rising, Rooted 63
The Day the Dead Rose 64
Holy Ground 65
Riveredge 66
Tell Me 67
Once More 68
In The Beginning 69
Who Can Explain 70
Visitation 71
River Way 72
Baptismal Prayer 73
Canal Du Midi 74
In Praise of Morning 75
Mystery 76
Peonies 77
Rutting Season 78

Acknowledgments 79

I

PLATO'S CAVE

Wasps sting,
but this one, dying,
seemed harmless,
trapped in a sliver of sun,
inches from the open door
where life lay waiting.
Though then again,
how could she know
when what she felt
was warmth enough,
that just the other side
of shadow, light,
unfolding, filled a sky.
As I, years later,
wonder why
I still remember
how she crept,
to that dark edge,
and back again.

WHITE PELICANS

One early spring in Illinois,
startled by the foreign sight
of pelicans upon dark water,
we stopped to stare, my mother,
and I, at such ungainly awkward
birds–the males with their red-
knobbed bills, flat drooping sacks
of wrinkled skin–watching as
they took to flight, laborious,
a clumsy sight, until, air-borne,
transformed,

and we, amazed, lay side by side
–though never touching, no, not that–
on soft new grass as feathered white
in dazzled light, they danced for us,
they soared and swung, angelic host,
they flew as one.

It's winter now, black branches stark,
my mother felled–a sudden stroke–
she sits, stiff-limbed, upon the bed.
I kneel to dress her. Socks, shoes, bra.
Her skin is soft. My fingers dance.
She lifts her arms as if to fly.

LAST WEEK IN JERSEY CITY

Only last week in Jersey City the Virgin Mary
appeared without warning on the freezer door
of a small Spanish market–or so I read in the
Boston Globe–her image lasting several days
as yearning pilgrims came to pray, kneeling
before stacked frozen food as Mary, dream-like,
disappeared, according to the *Globe*, that is, but
who am I to doubt such things? Improbable as it
may seem, burritos are real, and grief, and flowers
wilting in jelly jars left before the clouded glass.

PRAYING WITH LUKE

When you pray, go into your room, he said:
Each green dawn as spring light stirs, I sit,
womb-snug, in this small space, hushed high
above unfurling leaves with you, our Luke,
five days new but solid as a loaf of bread;
I hear you breathing, petal-soft, receive,
release. That's all. Enough.

EXCAVATOR

It's winter when the basement floods,
not once but twice, a bitter time,
taking out the heat, hot water.
The world shivers, children die,
why, we ask, obstruction hidden,
but it's clear the channel's blocked.

It's time to dig, to call upon the excavator.

Today they come, man and machine,
bright yellow on the crusted snow,
driver in the cab aloft directs the arm,
the hand that scoops, such gentle motion
back and forth as if determined not to hurt
but to uncover what lies deep, pipe that's
choked with roots, debris, lay bare
whatever blocks the flow.

CRAWLSPACE

I don't want
to go
down steep stairs
into the basement
belly
but am drawn
down
into
the storeroom stacked
with broken parts
scattered on plywood
Shelves not meant
to carry children
shudder as I climb up
to a hole
through which I crawl
into a space that smells
like death
is death   damp   dirt
dust   to   dust
Mother
where are you
in this womb
cocoon
nothing
is seen
it is utterly
dark
I lie
on my back
Only the smallest
child could sit
and I am twelve
my body

severed
numb
though whose
body
is it anyway
whose   yes   why
what happened
when who
took what
wasn't
theirs
to take
There is
too much
in this
crawlspace
coffin
where
no one
finds
me
I play
dead.

SNOWDROPS

In bitter cold, the grieving wait for
what might rise from shattered ground:
beneath the rubble, something stirs,
a baby, newborn, cord attached, alive,
beside her mother, dead, is lifted into
naked air. Like snowdrops deep in winter
dark, slipping through the frigid crust,
the unexpected slender stem,
the delicate white-petaled bloom.

WINTER SOLSTICE

Cradle of quiet,
trees wait, naked
on the hill,
the broken branch,
the body, broken;

nothing is hidden
snow has yet to fall
the grass lies mute.

It could be death but
isn't yet. Wings
quicken serrated air,
nuthatch, junco,
chickadee, flit from
tree to tree, oblivious
to the hawk circling
overhead, waiting for
what comes next,

and it will come
to all of us–there's
no exception–but
if that frightens you,
hold it like a stone
beneath your tongue
until it softens, and
light lifts shadows,

out of sight,
sap, wakeful, whispers
in the apple tree.

VERNAL POOL

Here nothing moves, water
waiting still as glass amid
the cattails' silent stalks, while
over there across the sea, fire
shreds the sky exploding as
buildings crumble, mired
in blood.

So how to hold the killing
field and this spring pool
where water shivers once
and wakes to the wood frogs'
rising chorus that, startled
by my presence, stops–only
to begin again?

THERE IS A FIELD

Love is the physical structure of the universe.
  Teilhard de Chardin

So, he said, but what is love?
A word, that's all, like 'tree'
for instance, one word to hold
the all of it, twig, branch, seed,
white oak, white pine, acorn,
resin, leaf or needle, fragile
birch or wild apple, roots,
of course, the inner life,
heartwood, sapwood, cambium,
evolving seasons, sleep and growth,
space surrounding, rain, sun, dirt,
eyes that see and hands that touch
the bark, the spark that animates.

BLACK ICE

Along the edge lace filigree shatters
at the slightest touch, shards scattering
like broken glass, but farther out the ice
is thick, immobilized by Arctic cold,
weight of water, locked down, trapped,
mute as stone, the weight of grief,
immutable, the weight of fear impaled
on the frigid air, but if you dare, it's there
you kneel, your face to ice, to watch
fronds sway and minnows glide,
the dearest freshness deep down things,
aquifer from which life springs.

CHAPEL OF THE BLACK MADONNA

It was there, on a crooked cobbled street,
my father joked that he, like Simon de Montfort,
killer of innocents he so admired,
should crawl on bony knees,
in penance, up worn granite steps
carved into that brittle cliff,
stairway to the Black Madonna.
I remember how we laughed
at such a thought, that such a man…
And how in that soot-shrouded chapel,
my father, strangely seized, bought
prayers for me
though he himself believed in nothing,
but he insisted so I accepted,
touched, perhaps,
by such attention, not knowing why
or what it meant when, later, in the car,
descending, without warning, he exploded,
shredding silence as I drove:
"Too fast," he shouted, "Damn you! Damn you!"

THE BEAUTIFUL BROKEN

Once lush trees on Quarry Pond
withered as the water rose to leave
the leafy island bare, black branches
broken, barren bone, bleak crosses
stark against spring sky.

But look! Great Blue Herons glide
across the pond to flutter down;
perched like blossoms on bare limbs,
they snap with sharp beaks slender
twigs, carried to their half-built nests.

Circling back to gather more, beautiful,
they drift, descend, wings outstretched,
to bloom again, and beautiful the feathered
trees, flowering of wounded wood.

RAVINES

Where I lived as a child the earth was flat,
no hills or valleys, only sky, though there
were trees, at least in town, oaks and elms
(before they died), trees to climb or hide
behind. But more than trees there were
ravines, cut deep, slicing silent streets,
slow streams of sewage, raw and steep.
In summer, stench rose as I crept through
slick black tunnels under roads, breath held,
heart pounding: a murderer, a man, I'd heard,
escaped from prison with a knife. It might
be true. I knew what lurked where children
slept, at night, at home, no place was safe.
And so I swung on vines that broke, and
walked on girders under bridges, hands out,
shaking. I hated heights but there was hope
that if I lived, I wouldn't die, and if I died,
I killed myself. Better than being stabbed,
I thought, by some man waiting in the dark.

DISPIRIT

To be low in spirit
is to watch rain
darken the cold
bare branches as
a friend lies dying
while another forgets
we were to meet
so that I, dispirited,
walk alone, haunted
by the hungry ghost
who knows too well
this empty place;
yet in the shadowed
sodden swamp, marsh
marigolds spark candled
light, and in the sky
at dawn today, the thin
moon held one burning
star.

INCLINE YOUR EAR

Imagine the shell you find
on the beach, a large conch,
half-buried, glistening in
morning light, waiting to be
lifted, rinsed, cupped

to your ear: This is your body,
listen and hear; blood flows,
pulse ticks, the ocean hums,
waves curl, crest, hushed foam
licks wet sand, thoughts rise,

dissolve, wind whispers shhh…
the body breathes, deep waters
rest as silence speaks in the cave
of your heart. *Incline your ear.*
Listen. Come to Me.

RAPID RIVER

Below the dam, the river roars,
savage in its steep descent,
racing as I walk beside it,
stumbling over roots and rocks,
while waves crush boulders,
splintered white, until, at last,
the slip-stream spills into a lake
of mirrored blue where water
quiets, smooth and deep.

It's here I always come to fish,
but first I rest, as if in prayer,
to still the mind, the wild thoughts,
rapid, thrashing, tumbling, quick,
until, with time, thoughts slow,
slip, settle in the place where
calm and chaos meet.

THE LAST MATTRESS

Yes, it was pricey, the salesman said
but the best investment we could make,
last you forty years at least, which though
I didn't tell him so put me at 110 with
my husband three years older; instead, I said
I didn't plan to be around though I hoped
our children would so one of them might
wish to have it, though then again it came
to me that this last mattress we will buy
might be the one on which we die and in
that case they wouldn't want it, a thought
I didn't share with him that we, in fact, were
buying our deathbed, a somber thought but
comforting to think that we might die at home,
wherever home might be by then upon
a mattress called the Cloud, appropriate, it
seemed to me and, pricey, yes, but worth
the money to sleep to dream… ah there's
the rub for what comes next no one can know
though I confess again it seems that in
the deeper sleep of death the breath of life
exhaled, returns.

MAUNDY THURSDAY

Clean towel, new socks, warm water
waiting, I kneel on Boston Common,
holding his naked foot that shows
what happens through a raw winter,
homeless, on city streets. This foot,
these feet, swollen, toes deformed,
skin cracked, I wash gently, and
never have I felt so close to Jesus,
his feet, bare, pierced, bloodied,
nailed to the wooden cross.

MOURNING

For Holly

In early March
the doves mourn
as each new dawn
I sit, looking over
the barren field
where for ten days
nothing stirs until
six weeks from
the day she died,
an owl flies from
dark woods to perch
on a bare branch
above the Buddha
where, motionless,
his round unblinking
eyes stare into mine
though who knows
what he sees, or what,
if anything, it means,
but life is like that,
isn't it, the way it
sometimes when least
expected breaks wide
open, and what appeared
as lost is found.

GREEN ANOLE AT MIDDLETON PLACE

Standing rooted, winter-locked, my hand
outstretched in southern sun, the lizard leapt
to the branch of my arm as if I was the tree
he sought, resting, weightless, green as grass,
throat-fan ballooning with each breath, and
I felt something ease inside, a sweetness rising,
as he ran, quick as raindrops, up my trunk,
toe pads tickling as he touched lightly, neck,
cheek, hair, like a blessing, like a prayer.

THE WRENS' LAMENT

Who knows why the fledglings died–
slowly–lingering even now in the nest
built in the clothespin bag hanging from
a nail on the porch while the frantic
parents sing forth their lament.

Was it the cramped contours of the bag
bristling with wooden pins, or our evening
presence on the porch, or the early laying
of six small eggs in this long cold spring
of frigid nights?

Why? And how can such liquid notes
purling like a mountain stream, be grief,
though watching the parents' frenzied flight,
the silent nest, the seed, uneaten, falling
from the mother's beak, how can they not?

This is not the poem I planned to write
when life cracked open the tiny speckled
eggs, but even now that joy remains within
the layered saddened heart as does the hope
that what has been will, surely, be again.

MARGUERITE PORETE

(author of The Mirror of Simple Souls, d. 1310)

It's June when she's burned at the stake,
lavender blooming in French fields, lilacs
beginning to fade, their honeyed scent
mingling with smoke as on-lookers weep
to watch flames licking her naked flesh,
but she doesn't flinch, she will not recant
even though this is the price she pays for
believing the Divine Spark, gifted from
birth, resides within each of us, nor does
she know that seven hundred years will pass
before she comes to light as the woman who
writes that *her Soul is so burned in Love's
fiery furnace, she feels no fire, for she is fire,
the fire of Love.*

II

SKI SWEATER

for Strachan

Don't be surprised
to hear me speak
for yarn like mine
holds memory well
over fifty years in
fact when she who
bought me turned
eighteen which means
that I am pregnant still
with winter's cold, steep
western peaks, sweet
scented woodsmoke,
sun-warmed skin, soft
feathered snow, stars
drifting dark, enfolding
arms of one now
dead embedded
in tight woven strands.

RANDALL

That's what they named him,
the barred owl who returns
each morning to perch on
the same branch of the white
pine, motionless until dusk
when he disappears into
the dark net of winter trees.

Those are the facts, but truth is
something else again, and each
day when I go to greet him,
I wonder what, if anything,
he's seeing as his dark eyes
stare, unblinking, into mine.

A rhetorical question, I admit,
but the older I am, the less
I know, the less I need to know,
and as for truth, isn't it enough
to simply be two living creatures
gazing, silent, eye to eye.

REFUGE

There was nothing, it seemed, to see
that day at Great Meadows Refuge
but lily pads like yellow cups holding
thin September sun. Lovely, yes, but
where was life? That's what I needed,
what I craved, for death and dying
encircled me. Smooth water slept,
an opaque shield. I stopped and stared.

The veil ripped; there, I see, a foot
away, a sandpiper who looks at me.
Closer still a turtle creeps, in liquid light,
green head held high. Where I'd seen
a barren spit, piping plovers, bobbing,
feed while dragonflies' translucent wings
fill living air with shimmering.

SEMIPALMATED SANDPIPERS
AT HOPEWELL CAPE

They were not why we stopped that day when driving up the Fundy coast:
Instead, it was the Flowerpot Rocks we'd read about and thought we'd see,
rose-colored arches, smoothed by tides, spectacular in rock-like ways,
but were they worth the twenty dollars we paid to catch a crowded glimpse,
we asked ourselves as we walked on (for having paid, how could we leave
and surely there was something more)? There was, we saw, a narrow walk,
a tongue of wood above the Bay where people huddled, hushed and still,
staring, though at what, we wondered, when easing back they let us through,
pointing to what seemed to be a nut-brown strip of speckled sand, shrinking
as the tide swept in. But how to recreate that day, that breathless moment
when we saw, instead of sand, a living mass, close-clustered, chirping.
Ten thousand birds, the young guide said, that each year fly here from
the Arctic to rest for six weeks, eating shrimp, gaining back the weight they
lost before they fly, non-stop again, three days and four nights to the Tropics.
Those were the facts. I needed them, but what I felt can't be described as,
suddenly, the birds rose up into the blue cathedral sky, a sheet of liquid waves
shook silver, shimmering as wing tips turned like poplar leaves in summer sun
now and now and now again, ten thousand birds that moved as one.

SUMMER PLACE

"Has it changed?" my brother asks,
the place he hasn't seen for years.
"No," I tell him, "No, not really,"
the house still overlooks the harbor,
the boats at anchor, trees, the sand.

Still, everything changes, doesn't it;
trees lose leaves, ice melts, glass
cracks, and all of us in time will die,
our bodies like a summer place
we dwell in for a certain season.

But I don't tell my brother this,
or how, one night, I swam alone
beyond the docks into the deep,
the lake a womb, to float in darkness,
naked, all my inmost parts.

PIETA

He was last to enter the small plane,
a tall man, ducking through the narrow
door, carrying a slight form hidden
beneath a cotton sheet, motionless
during the hour's flight, not dead,
I hoped, not yet, but sleeping, silent,
the man too, silent, head bent, listening,
as if waiting for someone to tell him
why, and why it is these long years
later, I still hold that cradled child?

STRIPPED

Late November, trees stripped
clean and what was hidden now
is seen, the path that leads into
the woods, the littered leaves,
the crooked walls that once
marked fields where grass grew
tall, remnants of a time long past,
reminding me that nothing lasts.

Will death be like this, do you think,
the day the breath does not return;
will our true nature be revealed when
stripped of memory, dreaming, sight,
will we, too, open to the sky, and, like
the forest, fill with light?

ON CUTTING MY FATHER'S FINGERNAILS

I bend forward, clippers poised.
Holding his hand, my fingers
tremble. He waits, impatient.
Cut, he says, but I am afraid of
cutting him, blood seeping from
old wounds, soiling the hospital
tray between us. My clippers click
on empty air. *Cut closer!* he says.

Out the window winter
light casts shadows
across deep snow. So
much lies buried, will
remain buried even when
spring softens the knife-sharp
branches on the tree.

I do not dare to speak the truth.

He does not see the child he hurt.
He has never seen her.
With her fingers, I tighten
my grip, and close to the quick,
I cut.

IF THE WORLD IS TOO MUCH WITH YOU

consider how the sun, each morning,
rises without being asked, or should
I say, appears to rise when, in fact
earth circles the stationary star,
spinning us along with trees and
butterflies into each new day, from
darkness into light, floating, all of us,
yet we stand upright, grounded,
our bodies too, each one a microcosm,
earth, air, fire, water, a symphony of
many parts, arms that lift, lungs that
breathe, eyes that see the radiance
of snow.

ETTY HILLESUM

(1914-1943)

There's no containing what
we call God, force-field of agape
love, within the seed, the star,
the sparrow, galaxies and grains
of sand, limitless without exception,
mystery beyond our knowing,
beyond and in all sons and daughters,
in those who show us how to live,
stripped of self to flower forth,
the desert blooms, the spark ignites
the Dali Lama, Desmond Tutu,
Rumi, Etty Hillesum singing, yes,
singing, on the train to the camps.

SPENDING THE MORNING FILLING MY FOUNTAIN PEN

Sitting by the river, hoping to capture
the day on paper as the cartridge draws
slowly, and water sings and trees bear
witness to the liquid light flowing as
the river flows, and time and ink,
flowing, fill the pen with everything
which doesn't take all morning; but
it could.

FRESH WATER

on a Catskill stream spills, flowing
down a smooth rock face into a pool
shaped like a cup held within high
rounded walls. A Chinese painting,
think of that, fine brush strokes forming
fissured cracks from which green ferns
unfurl lace while light falls feathered
through green leaves as I stand, dreaming,
rod in hand in what I know is sacred space,
when all at once the hatch begins. Mayflies,
caddis flutter, flying. Trout surface, sip.
The water wakes.

METANOIA

In June at dawn above the pond,
a snapping turtle blocks my way,
an armored tank, she fills the path:
grotesque, there is no other word,
the black-bead eyes, the cruel sharp
beak I've seen drag ducklings down
to death: And yet, not knowing why,
I sit, breathing slowly in and out, as
motionless, I study her, rough carapace,
reptilian claws, the savage smell of
mud, reed, swamp. She doesn't move.
She studies me. I watch a pulse beat
in her neck. We breathe together, in
and out.

MOTHER

She stands on edge
beyond the light,
her face in shadow,
locked so tight.
She lives inside
a pumpkin shell;
who put her there
I'll never know,
what darkness
trapped her,
who did what,
the key is lost.
Her eyes hold night.
She cannot touch.
I touched her once;
I was thirteen.
'Don't,' she said.
She pushed away,
Her voice was glass.
It shattered
me.

WHAT THE BONES KNOW

It was December when we walked, my mother and I
on brittle grass to find her friends, their names cut
into marbled stone, beneath a sky of chiseled blue.
We found their graves and, silent, sat, remembering
who they had been, wed in wartime like my mother,
stripped to bone, to what bones know, the secrets
we, the living, keep, like dreams forgotten as we sleep,
but locked in body, blood, bone, heart–long years
their husbands were away, the rough return, more
children born, hair permed, dress starched, mute table
set–who they were now beneath our feet, melting,
mingling, dust to dust, into the patient waiting earth.
Like Easter gifts I loved when young, small ribbed
seashells shuttered shut that placed in water slowly
parted, revealing flowers, stems unfurling, my mother's
friends ease open, rising, with all they held within,
released.

HOW EASY

they make it look
when after a hard frost
on a windless morning,
leaves let go with what
seems so little effort,
fluttering in slow descent
as if they trust what can't
be seen, the thin place
holding life and death
in this, the threshold of
the year.

TO FEED THE BIRDS

each morning, break the ice
in the stone birdbath,
water essential as suet
in this time of drought–
earth cracks, brush burns,
the crude beast circles
beneath the unrelenting sky.

Waiting, the world shivers.
Turkeys strut, preening.
Stars spin, hidden, but when
sun sets the full moon rises:
Without darkness, we would
not know light.

Despite the cold, let go, settle,
hand outstretched, palm open,
trusting that in time he'll come,
chickadee who dares to perch,
fearless, on your quiet skin,
to eat the seeds you hold for him.

WHY

Why did God make half a moon,
Lyle asked when he was three,
on the back steps, side by side
with me beneath the quarter's
quiet light. *I don't know*, I said
because I didn't, and still don't
know though Lyle now is in his
twenties, and I am old.

I could, I know, have told him
how the sun and moon and earth
create the half, the full, the waning,
but not the "Why" of moon or star or
mockingbird, or why the eel or
black-eyed Susan, or eyes or feet
or human beings.

That's the question, isn't it, why us
when given all we've done, genocide,
the ravaged earth, *erred and strayed,
no health in us*: And yet today in winter
light, a squirrel leaps from tree to tree
as easy as a bird in flight, sun licking
fur that shimmers silver, a rodent thief,
I know him well, but even so the heart
delights, arms lift in wonder, love, and
praise.

HORIZON

For Barry Lopez

There is this
boundary,
the thin place
between
two worlds
beyond which
we cannot
see but
nonetheless
we know
exists, and
if we dare
to climb
the highest
tree where,
clinging
to the topmost
branch,
we look
to the horizon's
edge where
light begins,
and there is
only sky, all
that separates
falls away.

BODY OF THE WORLD

When spring comes,
the body wakes, flesh
of our flesh without whom
nothing would exist.

Mother to all, raccoon,
fish, flower, no need
neglected, food, warmth,
water.

The body stirs, buds
quicken, sprout, green
softens hills, trees
blossom, fruit.

Womb in which
we have our being,
source of life, praise
her, praise him

FIREFLIES

It was midnight when we saw them,
we thought we must be dreaming,
night itself lit from within as if
the Milky Way had fallen, a multitude
of living stars illuminating rain-soaked
grass, the host of heaven come to earth,
beckoning, it seemed to me, and
I remember how it felt to rise, submerge,
to enter in that sea of luscious liquid dark,
our arms outstretched as if to swim
winged waves of incandescent light.

III

REUNION

The crush of bodies, bow ties, suits,
sleek smiling women dressed in silk,
din of small talk drowning thought,
and all I yearn for is escape, but where
to flee when all around the high-walled
room glass-fronted cases hold me trapped?

Or so I think, but there beneath the glass,
I find Thomas Merton, sacred friend, who
writes I read, to Rachel Carson, and there
beside him, she replies, and Annie Dillard's
Tinker Creek, typed pages inked, words
penciled in, and Henry Beston, Wendell Berry,
soul companions circling me to speak of
trees and roots and wings, the mystery
within all things.

FEATHER

*"...The feather flew, not because of anything
in itself but because the air bore it along..."*
   Hildegard of Bingen

It could have landed anywhere,
swamp or forest; instead, floating
on the quiet air, the tiny feather
down drifted, weightless, from
the open sky into my cupped and
waiting hands, cream-colored,
fragile, soft as milkweed, reminding
me, how, like the feather, we're carried
on the breath of God.

HALF-LIGHT

Waking to winter's dawn,
room drained of color
except for neon numbers–
6:14–blinking on the bruise
of the bureau against a pale wall

while out the window
a world shrouded, everything,
all of it, wrapped in gauze:

like Lazarus, I think, when
Jesus, weeping, called him forth,
and he woke from death, blinded,
his body bound by strips of cloth
that, like a chrysalis dissolving,
fall away as he rises to stumble
through darkness, stunned,
not knowing where he'd been or
what comes next, until he merges
into sudden sun.

AFTER

the snow, snow falls
again, white on white,
slow dissolution,
deer shadows drift
through shrouded trees,
where forest sleeps,
the stuff of dreams:

Who knows what's real–
it could be death,
not this, not that, not
either/or, but both/and–

Now the veil lifts,
bluebird and cardinal
flock to feed,
burst of cobalt,
flash of flame.

RED FOX

If, at the breakfast table,
I had not looked up just
as the red fox, burnished
coat glinting, scampered
past, white-tipped tail
carried like a flag, I would
have missed him. I would
have missed him if I'd slept
late, sneezed, or even blinked
which makes me think how
much I've missed because
of chance–if chance is what
it is–the life I might have
lived if I'd turned left instead
of right, responded no instead
of yes, walked through one
door, not the other. I'm not
complaining: I wouldn't have
it otherwise given all I would
have missed; this life, this love,
this trotting fox outside the window.

SPEECH

Seated before the woodstove,
tongues of fire licking the glass
door, I wonder what it was like
for the first person to discover
she had the power to subdue
the night by striking two stones
together, sparking tendrils of smoke
to rise from dead twigs, grasses,
watching fingers of flame quicken,
flickering, expanding.

She must have held her breath,
scarcely believing such things
were possible, a world not yet
imagined, circle of protection
opening to warmth in winter,
light in darkness, the scent
of meat, roasting, grains stirred,
thickening, faces lit by firelight
as she forms sounds, struggles
to tell them *This is what we need.*

ALCHEMY

Stone-cold, dawn seeps silent
into being revealing a shrouded
world; dead leaves litter forest
floors, bodies, the brittle streets.
Even the birds are mute, falling,
stiff as sticks from frozen wires.
From where is our help to come?

Lift your eyes to see sun touch
the tiptop of trees, twigs dipped
in amber, not the thin light of noon,
but thick, sweet, succulent, flowing
like honey in slow descent, turning
everything it touches, branch, trunk,
even the shriveled leaf, into gold.

SLOW WORK

I cross the rough terrain on foot,
not knowing where or when
the end, but called through forests
thick with vines, retrace, return,
approach the swollen river;
the dark swamp quivers, each step
a held breath, waiting, until quick
now, here, at last the open field,
the unencumbered winter light–
it's slow work, this giving birth
so late in life.

THE OTHER SIDE

The river wild, current
fierce against my legs,
feet unsteady; I watch
fish rising on the other
side, too far to reach,
each cast, line snatched,
fly dragged downstream.

Water deep between us,
there is no crossing over,
though I am old now;
sometimes clouds part,
sun striking trout who
leap, translucent, into
crystal air   beckoning.

ACORNS

For Sharon

Listening
to acorns drop
from the oaks
in last light of
late summer
to land out of
sight on the dark
forest floor,
I wonder how
many will find
their way into
the soil to root
in secret, waiting
for spring to coax
tendrils into
dangerous air.

Not many, I suppose,
life being what it is,
harsh frozen earth,
tangled roots,
the hungry squirrel;
even so there is
this tender rising,
slow, subtle, sacred,
soft as green skin
touched gently
for the first time,
warmed by sunlight
breaking through.

RISING, ROOTED

Now is the time
streets shatter,
smoke thickens,
men strut, clutching
daggers, fear shrivels
hearts.

Now is the time,
be still and listen,
rooted and rising,
sound of the sea
whisper, a murmur,
fluid and flowing.

Now is the time,
return to the source,
rising in water,
rooted in earth,
fertile and fragrant,
womb of creation,

Shekhinah is rising
hear spirit speak,
mother, daughter,
sister, wife,
Sophia is rooted,
time to give birth.

THE DAY THE DEAD ROSE

Today the dead speak,
    friends, relatives.
I am older now, there are so many–
    strangers too:
        Rilke, Mary Magdalene, Jesus.

To hear you must listen with the ears
    of your heart, the way I listened
  as a child, arms wrapped around
the slim body of the birch,
    ear pressed to the smooth skin
to hear sap whisper *You are not alone.*

HOLY GROUND

Easy enough, we think, when Micah tells us
there are only three requirements; *do justice,
love kindness, walk humbly with our God,* and
yet, we're flawed–like the knotted back of
needlepoint, the tangled threads, chaotic colors–
we lie, we cheat, we steal, as I did as a child,
writing in my key-locked diary at twelve,
'I know I'll go to hell' after stealing the paper
punch from Helanders, my father's Christmas
present, stolen goods that he too stole from me,
not that I knew it then, nor did he know
his present wasn't mine to give, but it's all
connected, isn't it, hurt and healing, dusk and
dawning–turn the needlepoint over to see each
thread connected, proclaim your broken body
as holy ground.

RIVEREDGE

*"Jacob dreamed there was a ladder…
and the angels of God were ascending
and descending."*
  Genesis: 28:13

If not alone on the cabin's deck,
listening to the river whisper,
open to day's light unfolding,
I would never have noticed
the tiny spider descending,
dream-like, thread unseen,
from high rafters overhead
to the summer grass below,
or, soon after, her return,
laborious, to where she started;
who knows why or for what
purpose, mysterious descent,
ascent, like Jacob's angels
as he slept, but *surely God is
in this place* of living water,
solitude.

TELL ME

how, as you lay dying,
too late to cancel
all that came before–
the rage, the grief,
the unforgivable betrayal–
the storyline dissolved,
and in that moment,
the unexpected grace;
we saw each other
for the first time.

ONCE MORE

I come alone to find the river,
changeless, changed, swollen
now by summer rains, deep
water, violent, rushes, roaring,
submerging grasses, saplings,
rocks, and I too changed,
infirmities increased with age,
joints swell, blood thins,
the future threatens, yet still
the longing to surrender, and
open to the cloudless sky,
the insect, lit by sunlight,
rising, winged and weightless–
this brief life.

IN THE BEGINNING

"Everything in the world begins with a yes."
  Clarice Lispecter

For Bishop Tom

In the beginning there is only *Yes*,
infinitesimal, infinite, invisible
seed sprouting in swirling dark,
slow integration, expanding,
extending, sudden explosion
into light–baby, blossom, universe,
all beginnings are the same– and
Yes to a world begun without words,
Yes to senses born before language,
bird song, shadow, skin touching skin,
Yes to Tom whose ravaged brain erases
speaking, reading, names, but through
hands cupped upon bent heads,
the unimpeded heart pours forth,
nothing to restrict the flow of *Yes*
in beginning and *Yes* in the end.

WHO CAN EXPLAIN

what holds me at the river's edge:
scent of water, or sound of liquid
slipping over stone, solitude, or
line, like breath, unfurling, or
the White Wulff, drifting, or that
moment when the hidden brook
trout, its crimson belly, rises, takes,
the sudden weight on slender thread
ignites, unites sky, fish, river flow
through me.

So, I wonder how it was that when
he met them by the sea, and all he said
was *Follow me,* they turned, it seemed,
with no regret, leaving boats and nets
behind, as if he was the fish they sought,
as if their hearts burned even then.

VISITATION

The facts are these: My mother, at 100,
died, released from her demented mind.
A cool June day in Illinois we gathered
at her open grave with hope for birds to sing
her home. She'd been a birder all her life;
we longed for warblers, bluebirds, buntings,
a symphony of wings and song, but heard,
instead, the mower's growl cutting grass at
nearby graves on one of which a sparrow sat.

The day after I flew home, I sat that evening
on the deck, wondering where she was now,
a woman of her generation, not given to
a show of feeling, a child who wished she'd
been a boy–boys had privilege, never girls.

I pondered this. I pondered her, wishing more
for her, for us, when suddenly a bird appeared–
one I'd not seen for sixty years, but as a child
my most favorite, black-cap, white vest.
Rose-breasted grosbeak, resplendent in his male
garb, lit on the railing, a foot away from where
I sat. He looked at me. I looked at him. That's it.
That's all. She flew away.

RIVER WAY

If you wait long enough everything
passes though you need to stay awake
to see the great blue heron bald eagle
osprey making their slow way above
the river stopping at times to perch
motionless on the tall dead spruce
across the way but everything always
eventually passes the river otter slipping
along the opposite bank mergansers
waxwings blue-winged teal trout rising
or not depending on the season the seasons
too and always the river that even in winter
flows unceasing ribbon of unfurling light
teaching me over and over again
how important it is to stay awake
because everything passes
every   last   thing.

BAPTISMAL PRAYER

This is the season when trees
stand naked, stamped in sharp
shadow on still-green grass.
This is the time between living
and dying.

Grant me an inquiring and
discerning heart,

The air turns cold, and, daily,
darker. Bucks snort, circling,
racks at the ready. Women
wait, weeping. Who knows
what comes next.

the courage to will and
to persevere,

A threshold time between hope
and despair. A thousand joys,
a thousand sorrows. There is no
escape from death. There is no
escape from life.

the spirit to know and
to love you,

Dusk comes early. The last leaf
lingers on the asters. Wind sings
in the willows. Suet hangs from
the redbud tree. The night stars
gather. Owls hoot, calling.

and the gift of joy and wonder
in all your works.

CANAL DU MIDI

We enter, and doors close behind us,
gears grinding like reluctant secrets
buried so long they've been forgotten
on this ancient pathway linking sea to sea.
Entombed in shadow, dull stone chills.
The boat stirs, a cradle rocking.

Will dying be like this, do you think?
Will smooth walls hold us, cupped
like hands, to lift us, light as feathers
rising, to where the waters meet as one?

IN PRAISE OF MORNING

To rise early is to wake to shadowed light,
the air translucent, a membrane on the lip
of change with everything a miracle,
the floor, solid underfoot, the leg that lifts,
the hand that holds the brush, the spoon,
the body sitting at the kitchen table,
taste of tea, granola, cinnamon, the flow of
color into form, the tree, leaf, the bluebird
at the feeder, small spark of sky.

MYSTERY

For Ned

I don't know why hummingbirds,
resplendent jewels we love to watch,
refuse to share with one another
the feeder with its plastic flowers
hung from clothesline on our deck;

nor do I know what night creature
plucked the blooms, revealing holes
through which he drank to leave
the feeder emptied, stained, dangling
from its fragile hook, or why I wrote

when we first met *This is the man
I'm going to marry*, thinking you were
like my father (you both were sailors
after all), not knowing then how wrong
I was, and how right to marry you, and

how these many decades later despite
the mystery that remains, I clean, repair,
refill the feeder, and sit with you in
evening light, delighting in the birds'
return.

PEONIES

Full-bosomed blossoms
shiver in the jade green
bowl, cream-colored
petals, rose-tipped,
soft as skin between
the fingers, drop
suddenly like water
breaking, such quick
release as if they know
there's nothing to hold
on to, that everything
in time lets go, making
room for what comes
next.

RUTTING SEASON

Each year leaves fall, the curtain rises,
the stage laid bare to naked woods,
brittle twig, the oak tree's massive
trunk. This is the season

each year, stage left, the big buck enters.
His crowned rack bristles. This is the season
the doe, diminutive, appears stage right,
oblivious to what comes next–

she is that young– this is the season
each year the play begins again,
revealing all that has been hidden,
the deer, the fear, the shattered heart,

and yet each year the stage expands,
becomes the world: this is the season
holding moss, mist, the softened shame,
the partridge berry's tiny flame.

ACKNOWLEDGMENTS

I would like to thank Don Martin, editor of the Poeima Poetry Series for his help with the manuscript, Kathleen Wakefield for her advice and guidance, and the editors of the following journals where many of the poems in *Body of the World* first appeared, sometimes in earlier versions, and with different titles.

The Anglican Theological Review: "Who Can Explain," "The Beautiful Broken"

The Christian Century: "Plato's Cave," "White Pelicans," "Praying with Luke," "Excavator," "Winter Solstice," "Snowdrops," "Vernal Pool," "There is a Field," "Black Ice," "Green Anole at Middleton Place," "The Wrens' Lament," "Maundy Thursday," "Marguerite Porete," "Pieta," "Ettie Hillesum," "Spending the Morning Filling My Fountain Pen," "What the Bones Know," "Fireflies," "Why," "Body of the World," "Reunion," "Feather," "Half Light," "Red Fox," "Speech," "The Day the Dead Rose," "Mystery," "The Other Side," "Peonies," "Stripped," "Mourning," "To Feed the Birds," "In the Beginning," "Baptismal Liturgy," "Riveredge"

The Christian Science Monitor: "Slow Work," "In Praise of Morning," "Rapid River," "Metanoia"

The Cresset: "Last Week in Jersey City"

First Things: "Incline Your Ear," "Acorns," "Fresh Water," "Rising, Rooted"

The Penwood Review: "Ravines"

Presence: "Holy Ground," "Visitation," "How Easy," "After," "Once More," "Randall"

The Sewanee Review: "Chapel of the Black Madonna," "The Last Mattress," "Summer Place"

Sojourners: "Semi-Palmated Sandpipers at Hopewell Cape"

SoulLit: "River Way"

The Southern Review: "Refuge," "Canal du Midi"

The following poems also appeared in Finishing Line Press: chapbook, 2016: *Natural Life with No Parole*, "Plato's Cave," "What the Bones Know," "The Last Mattress," "Summer Place," "How Easy," "Ski Sweater," "River Way," "Last Week in Jersey City," "Semipalmated Sandpipers at Hopewell Cape"

The Poiema Poetry Series

COLLECTIONS IN THIS SERIES INCLUDE:

Six Sundays Toward a Seventh by Sydney Lea
Epitaphs for the Journey by Paul Mariani
Within This Tree of Bones by Robert Siegel
Particular Scandals by Julie L. Moore
Gold by Barbara Crooker
A Word In My Mouth by Robert Cording
Say This Prayer into the Past by Paul Willis
Scape by Luci Shaw
Conspiracy of Light by D.S. Martin
Second Sky by Tania Runyan
Remembering Jesus by John Leax
What Cannot Be Fixed by Jill Pelaez Baumgaertner
Still Working It Out by Brad Davis
The Hatching of the Heart by Margo Swiss
Collage of Seoul by Jae Newman
Twisted Shapes of Light by William Jolliff
These Intricacies by David Harrity
Where the Sky Opens by Laurie Klein
True, False, None of the Above by Marjorie Maddox
The Turning Aside anthology edited by D.S. Martin
Falter by Marjorie Stelmach
Phases by Mischa Willett
Second Bloom by Anya Krugovoy Silver
Adam, Eve, & the Riders of the Apocalypse anthology edited by D.S. Martin
Your Twenty-First Century Prayer Life by Nathaniel Lee Hansen
Habitation of Wonder by Abigail Carroll
Ampersand by D.S. Martin
Full Worm Moon by Julie L. Moore
Ash & Embers by James A. Zoller

The Book of Kells by Barbara Crooker
Reaching Forever by Philip C. Kolin
The Book of Bearings by Diane Glancy
In a Strange Land anthology edited by D.S. Martin
What I Have I Offer With Two Hands by Jacob Stratman
Slender Warble by Susan Cowger
Madonna, Complex by Jen Stewart Fueston
No Reason by Jack Stewart
Abundance by Andrew Lansdown
Angelicus by D.S. Martin
Trespassing on the Mount of Olives by Brad Davis
The Angel of Absolute Zero by Marjorie Stelmach
Duress by Karen An-hwei Lee
Wolf Intervals by Graham Hillard
To Heaven's Rim anthology edited by Burl Horniachek
Cup My Days Like Water by Abigail Carroll
Soon Done with the Crosses by Claude Wilkinson
House of 49 Doors by Laurie Klein
Hawk and Songbird by Susan Cowger
Ponds by J.C. Scharl
The Farewell Suites by Andrew Lansdown
Let's Call It Home by Luke Harvey
Forbearance by Cameron Brooks
The Shapes Are Real by Jill Peláez Baumgaertner
Carnets by Kevin Hart

www.ingramcontent.com/pod-product-compliance
Lightning Source LLC
Chambersburg PA
CBHW051700040426
42446CB00009B/1222